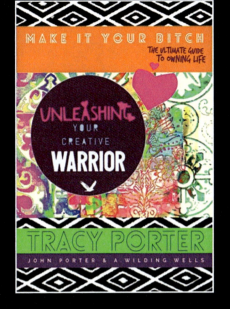

By Tracy Porter

With John Porter and A. Wilding Wells

Copyright 2016 Tracy Porter

All Artwork Copyright Tracy Porter

This work, Unleashing Your Creative Warrior (Make It Your Bitch: The Ultimate Guide To Owning Life), while a work of non-fiction, there are certain instances where names, characters, places, and incidents are products of the author's imagination or are used fictitiously. Any resemblance to actual events or locales or persons, living or dead, is entirely coincidental.

All rights reserved, including the right to reproduce this book or portions thereof in any form whatsoever.

For more information, please contact Tracy Porter at tracyp@poeticwanderlust.com.

MAKE IT YOUR BITCH

Unleashing Your Creative Warrior

THE ULTIMATE GUIDE TO OWNING LIFE

www.makeityourbitch.net
www.poeticwanderlust.com
www.awildingwells.com

dear creative warrior,
this book is for you because you have chosen to unleash your creativity and make it your bitch.
with love and explosive happiness,
xxx,
tp

You are creative because you say so!

And not for any other bullshit reason.

That thought will help you continue to push on when you need it the most. When you are down because you lost or you're broke or you didn't win the award or achieve the rank you set your sights on....that's when you will reach into your pocket and pull that thought out!

You are creative because you twist and turn and sparkle under the burning lights of criticism. And you swim when you feel like drowning. And you look in the fucking mirror and you nod even if tears are falling and you're filled with doubt and fear.

No one can take your creativity away.

There is no gatekeeper, no relation, no God. It's yours to own.

Now do it.

Get on with the process.

It's time to shine like a crazy Pink Floyd diamond.

My creative journey began when I was but a little kid. I was painfully shy and I wore these funky little blue horn-rimmed glasses that I easily hid behind.

Luckily, I am blessed with awesome parents who took note early on that my lack of confidence could have crippled me.

Making stuff is where I shined. It was always my go-to happy place...that along with going out to our barn and hanging out with the animals. I could get lost for hours in the barn or in creativity.

In truth, they were both creative endeavors. The barn was about me dressing up our cats in oddball outfits, or finding crap in our house to embellish the horses and play "costume".

I learned early on that not only did I love making things, I loved giving my creations away. I appreciated how happy it made me when I shared.

I still feel that way. See?

I still spend my days creating and messing with my animals, although not dressing them up so much anymore.

No one owes you anything. But you owe it to yourself to feed and nurture your creative soul.

Find value in your gifts and share them with others.

By the time I hit my teenage years my confidence blossomed in part to my creativity, and in part to my athleticism. My awe and wonder of the opposite sex was also soaring.

My grades though were plummeting, and the labels began.

"Math is not your strong suit."

"You're not applying yourself."

"You're not a good tester."

"You won't succeed if you don't get good grades."

The labels were not so much from my parents. They really never harped on my grades. They always told us the most important thing to do in life was to make sure you picked a career you would love to spend your time doing because you would be spending most of your life focused on that thing.

In short - academically, I was drowning; socially I was sticking the landings - 10's across the board!

Looking back, I wouldn't change a thing. I know that goes against what you might be thinking but, my loves, as I gained social confidence, other things began to happen. Important things that matter way more than grades.

I was no longer terrified to speak in front of the class, or raise my hand even if my answer was possibly wrong. I was finally able to stand up and put myself out there; I was brave enough. And that is everything.

Brave enough was – and is – massive.

Confidence in myself was what I needed, way more than good grades, or useless tests that reinforce negative labels and commit kids to boxes they may never escape.

I wasn't told by my parents I would not be successful because my grades sucked. Producing a correctly memorized answer was not going to make or break me in life.

The message in our family was, believe in yourself, be willing to try lots of different things, have balls and determination, try your best, work smart and hard, have hobbies, have fun and teach yourself to do new things all your life. That was it. Pretty simple advice.

I was not coddled or pressured to be an "A" student. I didn't need to be good at everything.
I still don't need to be good at everything. But guess what, I have balls and drive and confidence and I work my ass off even when I'm sometimes failing up. And, oh yeah, I fucking love it because it's mostly a shit-ton of fun and I decide how I spend every minute of my time.
It's the same advice we give our four boys. I would say any day to anyone: confidence and drive trumps grades. Don't confuse ego with confidence – they are not the same. Ego is meaningless inflated outside fluff that comes with awards and bogus labels colliding with self-congratulatory stroking along with a nice side of parental coddling.
Confidence is something you build from the inside. It's about being okay with who you are and who you are not. Unfortunately our current academic environment doesn't support this concept, since we all supposed to be good at everything. Tests prove it...right?
And "brave enough" means you're willing to see life through a different lens. It says, you're willing to put yourself out there. Which means more experiences and greater perspective. That is a million times more important than grades in this day and age.

My extended story can be found in the back of this book, and I'll be sharing little tidbits of it along the way as well.

The concept of Unleashing Your Creative Warrior is something I've worked at doing my whole life, and my twenty-five-plus-year career as a designer has given me a unique lens to see through and now share with you.

I am one person with one perspective, so as you read my thoughts please keep an open mind. Not everything will apply to you but hopefully in these pages a few things will light a bonfire of goodness inside you to take action.

On your mark. Get set....

You have to trust yourself

in order to trust yourself.

Winging it

    This is what you do when you lose courage and forget how to play like a child. You use your imagination like the wind uses objects as musical instruments to play across and make noise.
    Winging it is what you do when fear overcomes you, or when you're unsure about what to do next or, really, even how to do it, whatever "it" may be.
    Turn your head — or your whole body — and look into those harsh shadows and move...sideways or crawling or inching. Progress.
    Darkness is a beautiful place from which to create because on the other side of it is light. And in the light you find imperfections and tiny cracks to explore and force open.
    When my husband, John, and I began one of our first businesses we decided we wanted to design and manufacture hand-painted furniture and home accents. We were hardcore dreamers. Neither of us had one damn clue what we were doing but we were hungry.

We doodled designs and put ads in the paper for woodworkers, and then winged our way through the entire process. We didn't have a business plan or any sort of long-term thought-process but we took action and that was a start.

Was it perfect? Hell, no. Uh, no. We worked from an unheated chicken coop in the middle of winter in rural Wisconsin. John would wake up at 4 a.m., chop wood and start the small wood-burning space heater. I'd come out once the temp was above fifty, roll out my paints from the electric blanket that kept them from freezing overnight and I'd paint.

The colors we chose for our first collections were the same colors we used to paint the interior of our ramshackle farm house; we couldn't afford separate colors.

We were embracing some of the most stressful things in life — all at the same time: 1) we were up to our ears in debt; 2) we were just starting a business; 3) we had just moved from Chicago to rural Wisconsin; 4) we were rehabbing the house; 5) we had no jobs or income; 6) we had just gotten married; 7, 8,...new in-laws, no new friends, and it was winter. It was chaos times ten and winging it was everything. Fear was present but our excitement and passion and purpose trumped it, trumped everything.

WHAT WOULD YOU DO IF...

You had to create from a new place, a prompt you've never explored?
• If you're a painter look at science
• If you're a cook look at sculpture
• If you're a photographer look at writing
• If you're a writer look at nature

PROGRESS IS EVERYTHING IN CREATIVITY.

DO SOMETHING RADICAL

TAKE A LEAP OF FAITH.
IT'S SCARY, YES.
BUT SO ARE FIRST KISSES AND TOUCHES.
SO IS LOOKING INTO SOMEONE'S EYES HOPING YOU'LL SEE LOVE.
DO SOMETHING RADICAL LIKE CHANGE YOUR PROCESS.
OR USE A NEW MEDIUM.
OR START AT THE END AND WORK BACKWARD.
IT DOESN'T MATTER IF YOU'RE A SCIENTIST, A TEACHER OR A GARDENER.
RADICAL CHANGES FORCE THOUGHT,
WHICH BEGETS NEW IDEAS,
WHICH MEANS PROGRESS.
PROGRESS IS EVERYTHING IN CREATIVITY.
IT MEANS ACTION AND INVENTION AND SEEING.

Blow Your Mind!

WE TEND TO STICK WITH THE MATERIALS WE ARE MOST COMFORTABLE WITH.
WHY? BECAUSE COMFORT IS WONDERFUL AND SOOTHING AND EASY.
BUT IF IT'S THE ONLY WAY YOU DO THINGS THEN YOU WILL NEVER EXPERIMENT AND GROW.
GROWING IS WAY MORE FUN THAN COMFORT. GROWING IS LEARNING.

Endorphin junkies unite

Endorphin surfing is another really awesome free thing you have inside you.

Free, as in it's up to you to tap into that delicious kick ass group of hormones. There are lots of ways for easy entry. Exercise, laughter, chocolate, sex, music, spicy foods, aromatherapy, etc... AND, wait for it... Creativity! Yes, your endorphins are boosted when you are doing creative activities, which then diminishes stress. Surprise, surprise. I'm not a scientist but I am daily proof that all these things work. Not that I do them all at once – I'm not that creative. Not yet.

Endorphin binging thrills me and makes for explosive happiness, and gets me through stuff that's pissing me off. The other side is fear, the side I loathe, because I'm human and shit hits the fan now and again and I get frustrated because my super powers to control the universe aren't manifesting (whatever). And then I remember it's up to me to work through it. Around it. Get over it. Move the fuck on.

Endorphins surfing helps massively.

Fear loves people who do notihng.

WARRIOR THIS

- Doodle your way out of frustration.
- Practice irresponsible art once and a while, i.e. create at night while sipping a lovely libation.
- Create in the wee early hours instead of night or vice versa.

Here's the deal, the only fight you ever have is with yourself.

Self-sabotage

Saying I want to be creative isn't being creative. The difference is action.
Why resist? Why think anything other than 'I'm doing this'?
Are you waiting for the perfect time to begin? That's self-sabotage. Action will crush it.
You can't figure out where to begin? That's self-sabotage. Begin at the beginning or middle or end. Or solve it first then tear it down and figure out how you answered it. Creating comes in many forms. Sometimes it's solving a problem, sometimes it's an expression in the form of a story. Regardless, it takes action.
If you find it impossible to throw your whole self at creating, at least allow your heart to begin the process. Trust yourself and begin.

WHAT WOULD YOU DO IF...

YOU WERE ON AN ISLAND WITH ALL THE TOOLS YOU NEEDED TO CREATE AND YOU KNEW NO ONE IN THE WORLD WOULD EVER SEE WHAT YOU'RE CREATING? NOT SO SCARY NOW IS IT?

PUT YOUR PROCRASTINATION KING IN HIS PLACE

The "I don't have time" excuse is the most lame cop-out on the planet. Do you know how people get stuff done? They fucking do it.

They make their Creative Warrior shove the King of Procrastination right off his mountain and take his rightful spot at the back of the line.

Now for the I-get-you part. I do get you. Really, I do. But, the reality is, self-deception is procrastination's whore. And that is some ugly shit. Uncle daddy ugly.

Change it. Change your habits. Not simple, I know. I realize it's a million times easier to fall prey to distraction than it is to move something forward that you really want. Unless you really don't want it. Now that's an interesting thought. Hmmm.

I'm not going to get all psychology 101 on you and dissect your issues. We all have them. We could all commiserate on the why's and how's and what happened in our childhoods to make us who we are. OR... we can take tiny little steps to change and move forward.

SOCIAL MEDIA AND TV AND YOUR FRIENDS WERE NOT AVAILABLE FOR THREE DAYS?

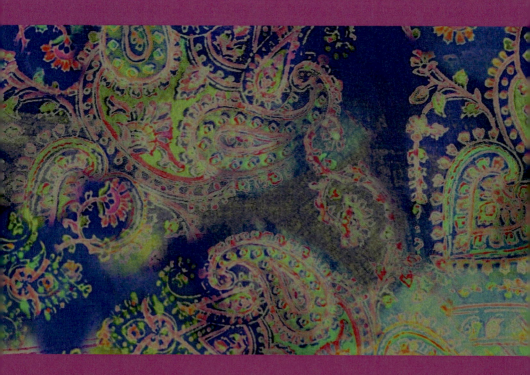

YEAH. I THOUGHT SO. INVENTING TIME ISN'T AS MAGICAL AS IT SEEMS.

Bumpy or not, travelling down new roads is always an adventure worth exploring.

SHIT HAPPENS...TO ALL OF US

SOMETIMES IT DOES FEEL LIKE YOU'RE TRYING TO EXIST IN A SHIT-STORM. AND WHILE WE CAN'T MAKE CHOICES ABOUT WHAT STUFF COMES AT US, LIKE A CONOR MCGREGOR LEFT HOOK, WE CAN DECIDE HOW WE'RE GOING TO DEAL WITH IT.

WHEN I WAS TWENTY-THREE AND OUR COMPANY WAS JUST STARTING TO HAVE SOME LIFT OFF, MY BODY DECIDED TO STOP WORKING PROPERLY. I COULDN'T LIFT MY ARMS OR ROLL OVER IN BED OR PULL ON MY JEANS. TAKING A SHOWER HURT; THE BAR OF SOAP PRESSED AGAINST MY SKIN CAUSED PAIN. I WAS SHARK-TANK TERRIFIED.

AFTER SEVERAL DOCTORS TOLD ME THERE WAS NOTHING WRONG WITH ME, I TROTTED OFF TO MAYO CLINIC FOR THREE DAYS. I HAD NO CHOICE BUT TO DEAL WITH MY HEALTH, EVEN THOUGH WE WERE SITTING ON SEVENTY-FIVE THOUSAND DOLLARS WORTH OF FRESH-FROM-OUR-FIRST-EVER-TRADE-SHOW ORDERS TO FULFILL.

I WAS A WRECK, YES. BUT MY HEALTH WAS EVERYTHING. IF I WASN'T HEALTHY THEN HOW WAS I GOING TO PRODUCE ALL THE ORDERS. WE HAD NO EMPLOYEES AND I WAS THE ARTIST WHO HAD TO PAINT EVERYTHING.
AFTER AN INSANE AMOUNT OF TESTING, I WAS DIAGNOSED WITH FIBROMYALGIA. IT HELPED ME TO KNOW THE THING THAT WAS STOPPING ME FROM FUNCTIONING HAD A NAME.
AFTER A LITTLE BIT OF WOE IS ME, I DID THE ONLY THING I KNEW HOW TO DO. I TOOK ACTION IN THE FORM OF BABY STEPS.
I ATE HEALTHIER. I EXERCISED MORE. I SPENT LOTS OF TIME STRETCHING MY BODY DURING THE DAY. I STOPPED WORKING UNTIL TEN EVERY NIGHT AND INSTEAD WENT IN THE HOUSE AND MADE DINNER AND HAD A GLASS OF WINE AT SIX. I FOCUSED ON MY RELATIONSHIP WITH MY HUSBAND AND WE DECIDED WE WOULDN'T TALK BUSINESS AFTER SIX. I READ SUPER INSPIRING BOOKS ON MOTIVATION AND SELF-HELP ALONG WITH BIOGRAPHIES OF ENTREPRENEURS I ADMIRED. I STARTED COLLAGE JOURNALING.

Blow Your Mind!

The next time shit happens that you have no control over reflect hardcore on what you can do to make micro changes in your life.
Then do them.
Shit will happen, be prepared.
Your creative warrior is inside you for a reason.

Obstacles...
Put the needle
on the record

So about that. Here's my two cents on training your brain to move beyond obstacles. It takes identifying and action and routine and evaluation. Are you sick of me yet? When I wrote my first novel (which, by the by, is no longer available as I pulled it off Amazon once I realized how sucky bad it was), I went through some brain training.

I decided early on that in order for me to write a novel (finish it) I needed to plant my ass in the chair and not overthink anything I was writing. Even though, on the other side of the door there were big hairy machete-wielding monsters. My inner critic was a bit nervous about people in the business world finding out I was writing romance novels that were decidedly raw and sexy. That one thought could have stopped me in my tracks. Hell, we have a family to feed that's dependent on my creativity. I cannot sabotage our income for two seconds. But I persevered and set that thought aside.

Then I considered my extended family and what they would think,...for like one blink. Yes, one. I quickly moved on knowing some of them would laugh and dismiss me and never read my books. Whatever.

Then I got hung up on my crappy grammar skills. And by crappy I mean scary bad. Maybe as bad as my math skills. But I know myself rather well; I learn by applying. I learn by doing. I knew I would get better if I hunkered down and didn't overwhelm myself by my lack of skill. I decided I could double-whammy combat my fear by finding a great editor who would be okay with a writer who sucked at grammar. I was turned down by several, but then found a great editor, and then another. And, I'm learning how to get better. I'm actually pretty damn good now.

IT'S NOT NATURAL FOR ME
TO CONSIDER RULES. I
STRUGGLE HARDCORE WITH
GRAMMAR AND ALL THE
TENETS OF WRITING. ON
THE GOOD SIDE, MY BRAIN
IS A WEALTH OF IDEAS AND
I LOVE WRITING SO MUCH
THAT NOTHING WILL STOP
ME FROM DOING IT.

THAT'S A LOT OF BRAIN
TRAINING.
BUT IT REALLY WORKS.
I'M PROOF.

WHAT WOULD YOU DO IF...

THERE WERE NO RULES AND YOU COULD CHARGE FREELY INTO YOUR CREATIVE BLISS?
AS OF TODAY ALL RULES ARE GONE.
UNLEASH YOUR WARRIOR.
BEGIN.

Let's face it, no one is going to call you an idiot for not writing a book

Pixie dust

Let's chat muses.
Are you waiting for creative muses to magically wend their way into you via the wish you blew out to the universe? Or are you unleashing your creative warrior and hunting muses down like they own your soul and future and key to explosive happiness?
Just to be crystal clear, either one is fine and spiritually personal.
I always go with my creative warrior. I prefer action, as it always leads me to more possibility and creativity. I really prefer taking responsibility for my creativity.

It's not that over the last twenty five plus years – while making a living as a creative – I haven't tried the pixie dust option. Yes, I tried. I worked to connect my inner fizz and four-dimensional quantum energy to my meridians of consciousness and circuit of vibration fields. But I kept slipping on the bullshit in the fields and then I ate the shit – hated the taste – and realized the only way to find my creative muses were to hunt them down and own them.

Hey, I'm just a girl. I have to work hard to make money, I have to take action. My nonexistent trust-fund states clearly in its nonexistent contract that working hard is my only ticket to Museville.
I'm sorry if that isn't a-muse-ing to you. Stick with your woo-woo if you want. I'll be over here charging forward riding the wings of my muses that I've harnessed to fly me around 24/7. Oh, yes, I do – I make my muses my bitch(es).

WARRIOR THIS

Creativity is not about talent. I'm honestly not exactly sure what it's about besides explosive happiness and my meal ticket. But, I do believe it's partly about setting aside fear in exchange for freedom of soul fulfillment. Are you able to do this? Do you need it real, real bad?

Authenticity makes the world go round

Does that sound fat and fluffy? It's not, if you think about it.
When you are willing to be authentically you, all pretenses are dropped. You become beautifully transparent and unafraid to expose your vulnerabilities. You let others see the real you, and often they too will open up and show you the real them. Imagine if the world could function with that level of trust.
So how does this relate to you and creativity?
If you can be velveteen-rabbit real in a world of fakes and filters, you won't be concerned with how you look to others because you'll be so busy looking with an open mind at everything's potential. Every word, every texture, every shape and imperfection will become an new source of inspiration.
Our first book which we wrote many years ago is still one of my favorite creations we've ever made. I was so confused as to why a publisher would want us to write a book, but after they explained we could make it what we wanted, everything made sense. They wanted authenticity. They wanted our raw story, and raw it was. Still is. I'm not much for sugar-coating. It was all heart and imperfection and it sold well because of it.
You can't invent authenticity, you simply have to be it. We all have it in us, it's a matter of dropping your mask and being cool with the beautiful you that you are!

Creating is healing, cathartic and mind-blowing when you free yourself and let it happen.

Blow Your Mind!

Cherish and nurture your creativity like you do anyone or anything you love
and it will reciprocate and grow and give and expand.
The ocean inside you is endless and deep and delicious.

Sexy Vulnerability

Odd combination isn't it? I never thought of those two words as a good thing until a friend of mine recently told me his favorite thing about the videos I create is how sexy my vulnerability is. I blushed, then considered his thought. I liked how he put it... sexy vulnerability. And truth is I can see that in other things and people, and he's right, it is sexy. It's sexy because real is sexy and people are so fucking afraid to be called on the mat that it's easier to put up a fake wall.

Being creative is being vulnerable. And, now that it's been couched in sexy... it's cool, right?

You are sexy because you're willing to be vulnerable and explore your creativity. Just don't let it go to your head, or become too sexy for your cat (too sexy for my cat, poor pussy, poor pussy cat - I love that I can drop a Right Said Fred reference in here!).

Blow Your Mind!

CREATIVITY IS A STATE OF MIND YOU CAN STEP INTO LIKE A SECOND SKIN AND LIVE IN ALL YOUR LIFE. DON'T TURN IT ON AND OFF, LET IT BE ALIVE INSIDE YOU ALL THE TIME.

Size doesn't matter...
in some things.

Creativity can come out in spurts and stops. Sometimes it comes out gushing. The next time it might squeeze out of a pore in a puny drip that might not fill the tip of a pin. In the case of creativity size really doesn't matter.
What matters is doing. Doing is pushing. Sometimes it means stopping and taking a breath to reflect. Other times it means starting over, or backing up.
It's different for everyone but it's great to know you are not alone in your pursuit.
There's a certain comfort in the togetherness of the idea that movement – not size – is what will keep you growing and loving the process.

WARRIOR THIS

Create when you are happy or sad, broke or flush, vulnerable, frustrated or even scared. Create in lies and in truths. Just create... greatness will be born.

Commit to being an experimenter

Try experimenting and watch yourself stumble into worlds inside of you that you didn't know were begging to be opened and explored.
Yes, try it in everything you do. Be an experimenter when you cook, when you eat, have sex, write, read, converse, listen, touch, feel. Imagine what you will unleash.
Even creative people shut some parts down. We are taught by limits and rules. Conformity in all areas of our lives is expected. So what?
Game on? Yeah, I thought so. That giddy thing you're feeling right now, was you agreeing with yourself that it's cool to want more out of life. Experimentation is part of it. Bust out and be free.

Blow Your Mind!

Being practical when creating will get you nowhere. Indulge your creativity. Think wicked and wild, be fascinated by everything, from the textures on a leaf to the beads of water on dewy cobwebs.

Kaleidoscope lens switch

Being creative is a way of life. It's not a thing you turn to when you're ready to shift gears. Anyway, I don't think it is. It's a way of looking at everything through your own unique lens. And the wonder of it is, you can choose the lens. Think of the possibilities. Lenses come in all shapes, sizes, colors, patterns, scents, tastes, noises. Why the hell would you choose the same lens?
That would be like eating the same food every day. How boring.
It's a choice! Your choice. Invent lenses. Try on someone else's lens. Layer lenses. Mix musicians with writers or scientists with painters. It's endless. Create your own mix tape of life.

WARRIOR THIS

The Flaubert + Coco Chanel lens.
The Madame Cury + Picasso + Maya Angelou lens.
The Jim Morisson + Steve Jobs + Martha Graham lens
The Beethoven + Thomas Edison lens.

BE STARVED AND THIRSTY

HUNGER AND NEED GO A HELLUVA LONG WAY WHEN IT COMES TO UNLEASHING ONE'S CREATIVITY. REALITY IS WANTING SOMETHING AS MUCH AS YOU WANT YOUR NEXT BREATH, AND IT'S PRETTY POWERFUL SHIT.

SOME PEOPLE WANT TO LIVE CREATIVELY 24/7 WAY MORE THAN OTHERS. IF I WERE IN A JAIL CELL, I WOULD BEG FOR PAPER AND A PEN. I CAN RUN CIRCLES AROUND SOMEONE WHO MIGHT HAVE FIVE HUNDRED TIMES MY TALENT BECAUSE I RUN STARVED AND THIRSTY NON-STOP FOR LIVING CREATIVELY.

IT'S SUCH A COOL THING TO ME. I GET THIS LITTLE BUZZY THING IN MY CHEST, LIKE A NEW LOVE HIGH THAT I CATCH AND RIDE. AND SINCE I DO THIS ALL DAY AND MOST OF THE NIGHT, IT'S A NEVER-GOING-TO-END FEELING. IT'S NOT EXHAUSTING...IT'S EXHILARATING.

I MAKE IT HAPPEN BECAUSE I WANT IT THAT BADLY. AND IT FEELS THAT GOOD.

HHELLUVA LONG WAY WHEN

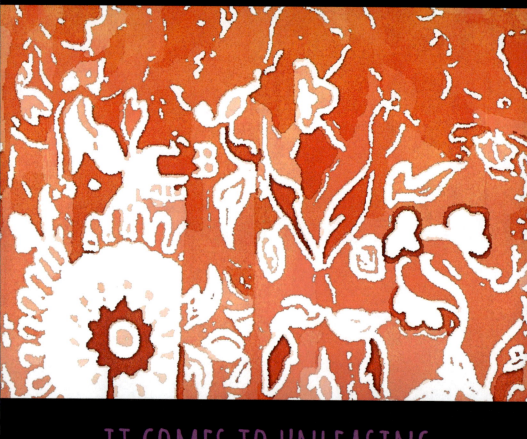

IT COMES TO UNLEASING ONE'S CREATIVITY.

WARRIOR THIS

LET YOUR CREATIVITY FLOW. YOU DON'T NEED TO KNOW WHERE IT'S GOING, YOU JUST NEED TO LET IT BLEED FROM YOU. CREATING IS HEALING, CATHARTIC AND MIND-BLOWING WHEN YOU FREE YOURSELF AND LET IT HAPPEN.

Orgasmic creativity

This goes hand-in-hand with the whole be hungry thirsty thing, but it's the sexy part. Do creative orgasms exist? Indeed they do. And just like sex, you need to let yourself go and be in the moment and feel free to explore and not feel judged. Sex and creativity have a shit-ton of similarities as far as I'm concerned.

They are about the here and now. They both involve foreplay, thank god. You have to get naked and be okay with vulnerable. There is fantasy involved, along with trust and the need for security and surprise.

Orgasmic creativity is beautiful and healthy and shameless, but it takes an open mind and heart to get there. It takes looking inside oneself and letting go.

Create your own mix tape of life.

WARRIOR THIS

Creativity is made up of little bursts of thought that all connect for an outcome. Sometimes it's brilliant; sometimes it sucks. If half the time it works, are you an F student? No! Half is brilliant. Half means you are jamming hardcore.

We (you) are a gazillion times more capable and creative than we allow for. Damn those doors and impenetrable fictitious walls we put up, that imprison us in tiny unimaginative rooms, with no exits.
It really is such a pathetic thing when you think about how massive our brains are.
Change the conversation.
Envision a room filled with millions of doors. Behind each one is a delicious path filled with bountiful elements all for the picking.
That's the fantasy to begin with.
If you need one, imagine a guide behind each door, your very own creative dossier.
Surprise yourself and let this happen... stop closing doors. Surprise yourself and your well of creativity will become a geyser. Then all you'll need is an umbrella because your creativity will rain on you until you're soaked and shivering in orgasmic pleasure.
On second thought, screw the umbrella and enjoy the climax.

Blow Your Mind!

Creating is not a brain tumor.

TAKE IT PERSONALLY

Make it your art. By that I mean climb so deeply into what you are creating that you lose all time and become as close to one with your creating as possible. Once you get this feeling a few times - an all-encompassing tow of creativity - it will happen regularly.

How do you get there?

Depends on what you're creating.

It's different for everyone. For me, when I write, I need to shut out the world of noise as much as possible. Not an easy thing to do when you live with five guys and three of them are teenagers plus one wannabe (you get to figure out if it's my ten-year old or my husband). I work to minimize sound so that the only noises I hear when I'm writing are the characters' conversations.

On the other hand when I make my designs I prefer to have music on. My process for these things is so different, but one thing is the same; I go in deep and I come out the other side feeling very accomplished with creating every single day. This is because I know I'm not cheating myself of the opportunity for full immersion. And that means I'm creating at my purest level. It might take me an hour or more to find my super zen. But I know when I'm there, because that's when the really good stuff happens.

You know when you're making good stuff...you just know.

I take my creating personally and I'm authentic with it to the core. Years ago, we did a licensing deal with Kohler. Yes, the plumbing products Kohler. Mr. Herb Kohler wanted to meet me. I'll admit this blew my mind since they were a six billion dollar company at that time.

His arrival was announced and, while everything felt a bit pomp and circumstance, he was lovely. When we talked I didn't shy, I shined. I knew the second he walked in the room and everyone scattered like minnows to the edges, there was no chance I was going to do that. I'm so glad I didn't back down. I have nothing to hide, nothing to fear. He's just a man.

And I'm an authentic woman.

WARRIOR THIS

NOW AND AGAIN, JUST SAY FUCK IT. FUCK IT AND MOVE ON.

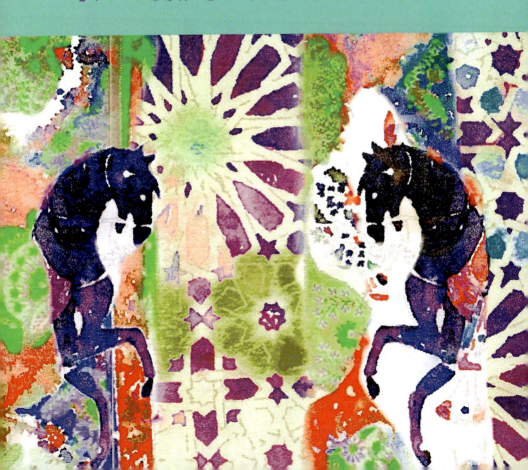

BLOWING DOWN THE HOUSE THAT FEAR AND ANXIETY BUILT

FEAR, AND THE HOUSE IT LIVES IN, HAS TAKEN CLAIM IN EVERY ONE OF US. IT'S THAT LITTLE PATHETIC SHITHOUSE YOU WANT TO DYNAMITE INTO A BAZILLION SHARDS OF NOTHINGNESS.

THAT HOUSE MADE OF FEAR AND ANXIETY IS YOUR PERSONAL NIGHTMARE BECAUSE IT CAN PARALYZE YOU AND SUCK YOUR CREATIVE JUICES DRY.

HOW CAN YOU OVERCOME IT?

MOVE TOWARD IT WITH YOUR WARRIOR. RIDE INTO IT WITH A FULL STEAM OF KOWABUNGA! AND TRAMPLE IT. NO MATTER HOW IMPOSSIBLE IT FEELS, YOU HAVE TO MAKE THE MOVE. YOUR BRAIN WILL LOVE YOU FOR IT, AND IT WILL GROW BECAUSE OF IT.

IT WOULD BE EASIER NOT TO TAKE RESPONSIBILITY.

LET'S FACE IT. NO ONE IS GOING TO CALL YOU AN IDIOT FOR NOT WRITING A BOOK OR NOT MAKING THE DISCOVERY OR FOR NOT SINGING THAT SONG ON FACEBOOK LIVE OR NOT DANCING ON THE STAGE OF LIFE.

ANXIETY WANTS YOU TO STAY IN THE DARK CORNERS OF YOUR BRAIN SO YOU'RE NEVER CRITICIZED FOR PUTTING YOURSELF OUT THERE.

It wants you to think it's safer there, even though it feels like acid in your gut.
It's a choice. You fight. Or you stay in the house and let it lock you in.
Fight means action.
Stay in the house and succumb to fear and anxiety means the opposite; do nothing.
Fight means progress.
Stay means get nothing, except a shit-ton of more stress for doing nothing. Weird right?
When we first decided to start licensing it was the early days, when company's rarely licensed with artists and their art brands. Everything was about sports figures or movie stars or dead guys. We were told by THE top New York agent that it was impossible for an upstart company in rural Wisconsin to make it in licensing. Now, I don't particularly like it when authority figures tell me no. It's high school all over again. So we jumped in naively. It was bumpy and scary at times, and there were plenty of industry folk that couldn't wait to put us in our place for being hick newbie's. But in time and with patience and persistence and much up-failing we made a nice name for ourselves.
It might have been more comfortable to agree to that pompous finger-wagging authority who wanted to push us down but what fun would that have been? Bumpy or not, travelling down new roads is always an adventure worth exploring.

Blow Your Mind!

Fight for your creativity. The first step is self-belief in your value.

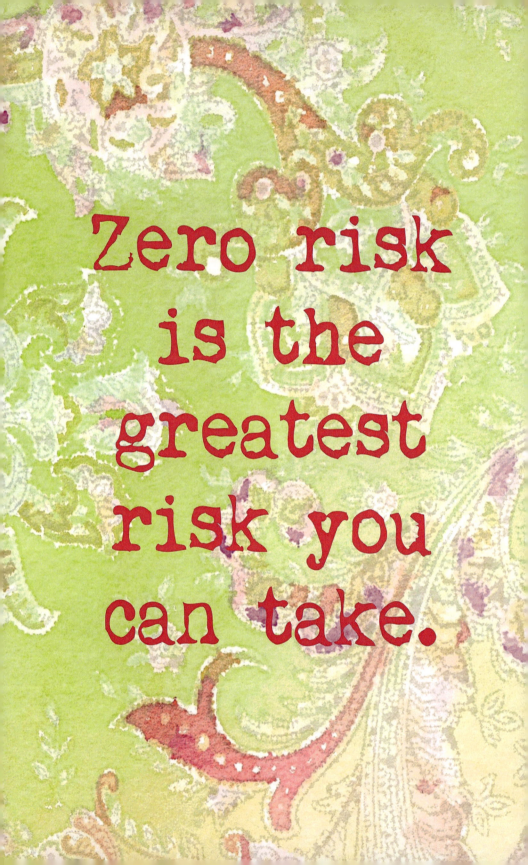

Self-Trust

I attach all kinds of stuff to that delicious little phrase, and all of it is candy to my soul.

When you have self-trust you are more open to your creativity, and less willing to succumb to bullshit "truths" about your inabilities.

I have no degrees in design or art or writing or anything. What I do have is self-trust and that's why when I decided to design everything from furniture to apparel to shoes, I was able to jump in and unleash my creative warrior.

I don't believe that because someone has a degree in any of the above, they are going to find more success than me if I jump into the ring and fight for myself.

I will fight harder than anyone because I believe in my perseverance and in my abilities to learn and grow and take steps. Who cares if anyone doubts you? They aren't the one doing the work. They aren't the one who wants it more than their next breath. They aren't inside your brain.

You can't control everything. In fact there isn't much you can control except self-trust. And with it, you can accomplish so much if you are willing to work for it and take steps and evaluate as you go.

WARRIOR THIS

Creativity is not about conformity. You need to get more than a little weird to slay dragons.

Speed has nothing to do with it

Fast or slow, work at your pace. You are only competing with you. Some people write ten thousand words a day. Some people can't write that in fifteen years.

It doesn't matter.

What matters is you are working and moving forward. And hopefully growing. It's hard in the 24/7 world we live in not feel like we are racing against time. I'll admit I do feel this way often. For me, I suppose it stems from my need to create more. Why? Because I find creating to be about the coolest thing on earth. It's invigorating. Even in moments of aggravation I can always find my center and balance if I create. Some days I produce slowly, other times I am a hurricane. Regardless, I'm taking **ACTION.**

Blow Your Mind!

Come back to your work. I tend to have multiple projects going at once. The one I'm working on owns me, body and soul. I stay present with it. That doesn't mean I finish it in one continuous movement. In fact, I find when I walk away to finish another project, then come back to an unfinished one, my perspective grows. Every creative project I do pushes the others.

Quality and quantity

Everyone has their methods for getting to the good stuff. The creative meat is gold.

Bottom line, I'm a producer. I'm also an editor, because not everything I do is marketable. I know this because I have been marketing my work for over twenty-five years and because I have sold my designs to most major retailers and thousands of boutiques as well. I have a pretty good feel for what sells. But I'm not cocky about it. I've been wrong too many times to be cocky.

How do you develop a feel for gold? You pan through a shit-ton of stuff and go with your gut on the things that shine.

My work has a very distinct feel, so I know how to navigate through the thousands of pieces of art I create to narrow it down to the best goods.

I've learned one thing in figuring out how to find the gold. I trust myself.

Once you surrender to your trust the road gets a little easier and more doors open. Trust comes with courage and patience and instinct. And as wonky as it might sound, you have trust yourself in order to trust yourself.

F is for Fail

In our current academic grading system an F grade means you got less than fifty-nine percent correct. You failed.
You rarely meet a creative in any field who will say they get half the things they tried right. In fact, I would call that individual who says they do get half right a unicorn. I was going to say liar but that sounds mean and finger-pointy.
Most people are getting F's. Hell, the best baseball players in the world are all failures!
If I get half of what I do right I am positively stoked out of my gourd.
F means I'm trying like crazy to explore new ideas. F means I've opened doors and moved things forward. F means I evaluated and I grew. F means I am busting my ass unleashing my creative warrior.

F means fan-fucking-tastic.

indulge

your

creativity

Leave the outside forces where they belong...OUTSIDE!

There are so many forces we can't control with our business. We have licensing partners, agents, buyers, customers and a thousand layers between each of those.

I have no problem with constructive criticism because I'm confident I can mostly weed through the difference between the pearls of wisdom and the bullshit.

That is not something that comes easily. I'll admit, I have snapped at people more than a few times over the years when their holier-than-thou wisdom soup they swim in is dumped on me because of their own insecurities. We're all human. It's okay to drop your basket now and again. Just know after you do you've got to keep creating because if you let the outside forces make you question what you're doing it will eat away at you layer by painful layer until your self-belief is nothing but a skeletal version of itself.

Blow Your Mind!

Remember this: No one cares about your struggles. No one wants to hear you whine. Move forward and you won't have time to bellyache.

Being creative
is
being vulnerable.

Feed your creative soul

There are many ways to nourish and nurture your creative soul; I would put attitude high on the list. If your attitude is in the right place – open, trusting, growth mind-set, optimistic – your exploration of your creativity will be that much more fulfilling. If you are able to view attitude as a way to nurture your creativity versus more tools and stuff and distractions and input then you won't need much of anything else. You'll realize how sated you are knowing your outlook is one of 'yes, I can have this, yes, I need this, yes I'm going after this'. No one owes you anything. But you owe it to yourself to feed and nurture your creative soul.

It will reward you time and again, year after year.

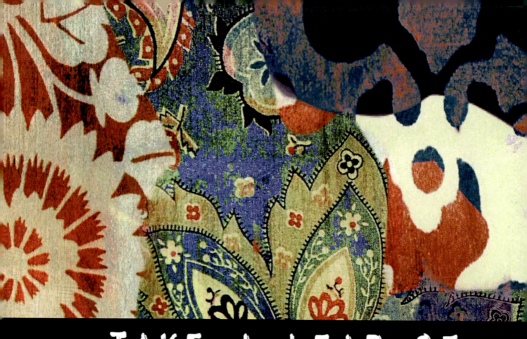

TAKE A LEAP OF FAITH. IT'S SCARY, YES. BUT SO ARE FIRST KISSES AND TOUCHES.

Finding wanderlust in yourself

Ironically, the more I create the less need I have for outside stimulation. I'm sure this sounds counterintuitive. But it's not. I find so many paths, windows, crossroads and untraveled terrain when I create that I'm infinitely satisfied.

I can easily write for fifteen hours. I immerse myself in a world so vivid and real to my imagination that I feel everything I'm creating. And I mean everything. It's that intense. It's as though I've stepped into a new world and slipped into the characters' souls.
I don't know how else to explain it, but it's pure human and beautiful. In its very essence, creating is truth.
If you can commit to it and practice your skill and immerse yourself everyday with full surrender then you will eventually find your inner wanderlust.

WARRIOR THIS

Lots of creatives say coming up with ideas is torture and getting them on paper is painful. Change the conversation and call it 'playing' next time creating causes you angst. That way if everything falls apart — like it sometimes does in life — you have the energy to deal with real torture.

Getting in the zone

Creativity is about living large and being in the moment where you are creating.
So why not create from this place all the time?
Is it because little things get in the way of movement and free thinking?
There are thousands of examples of rules you've been educated to follow, i.e. brush strokes you've been taught that should be "just so" and nothing else.
Sometimes we have to unlearn. We have to delete or erase rules and commands and how-to cages in order for us to surrender to the freedom creativity demands.
Technique is wonderful but it can get in the way of learning how to become more creative. You can and should always strive to become better and more skilled, but work first to be creative.

Blow Your Mind!

I'm sure some of what I'm saying might make you uncomfortable. So what! Creative warriors don't function in comfort zones. Blow your mind and get way the hell out of your own comfort zone. What might begin as pain will eventually turn into pleasure and power and explosive happiness.

WHAT WOULD YOU DO IF...

You never doubted yourself?
Don't let doubt rule your creativity.
It will steal all of it right before your eyes.

P.S. None of us know what we're doing

The emperor has no clothes. I love that tale so much because only children will say the obvious aloud. No one else wants to look stupid and think they don't see something everyone else does.
Anyone who is creating in any field is surprised on a regular basis by how much they don't know.
The beauty of admitting we don't know what we're doing is the freedom it offers. You can approach everything naively. And when you do, you tend to see things more clearly.
I have no law degree, but over the last twenty-five years I have easily learned to see what our lawyers and other consultants cannot. My view is so pure and childlike, in certain situations that I'm able to ask the stupid obvious — and sometimes really annoying — questions other people (experts) won't. And it cuts right to the core.
It's okay to keep figuring things out. Everything evolves.

CREATIVITY IS NOT ABOUT TALENT.

FIZZ WITH IDEAS

That sounds festive, fun and simple because it is. Or at least will be.
I'm not saying all your ideas are going to be gems. But they will get you forming a necessary creative habit. The routine of being an idea inventor.
Why does this matter?
Because ideas are everything. Save for action. Ideas are the perfectly fitting pieces in a world full of puzzles that need solving.
Let ideas flow. Capture them in whatever way works for you. It might not be a pretty process to begin with but don't let it intimidate you. If fifty tiny sticky notes sounds less scary than a pad of white paper then go that route. If collecting random objects that speak a language to you gets you going, start there.
Idea generating is worth doing every single day. Because when you're in a slump you can count on the fact that you're capable of coming up with creative ideas to get out of it.

WHAT WOULD YOU DO IF...

There was no one to tell you who you should be? What you should do? How you should be creating? Why you should listen to them? There will always be someone who wants to tell you what to do. Shut their noise out of your world and be true to you.

The magic of creativity

I tend to use the word magic pretty freely when it comes to creativity because, well, there is a certain magic in creativity. By that I mean the enchanting, spellbinding, hypnotic feeling you get when creating.

There are plenty of ways to get there. Note how I wrote "get there", not "let it get to you".

Yes, you make the magic. It's all up to you. And the routes to getting there are infinite.

Making magic is about seeing things from a fresh perspective and grabbing hold of it while it dances in front of you.

Blow Your Mind!

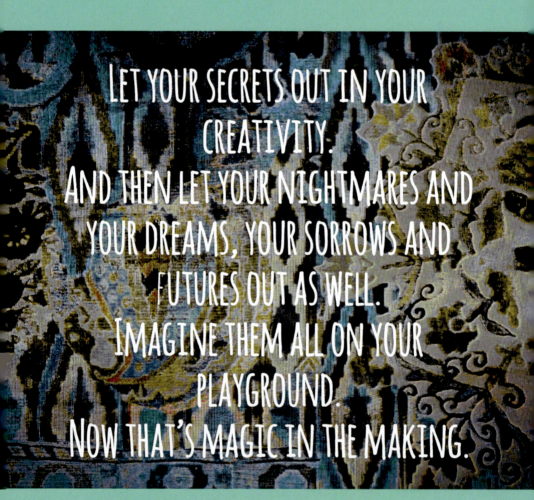

Let your secrets out in your creativity.
And then let your nightmares and your dreams, your sorrows and futures out as well.
Imagine them all on your playground.
Now that's magic in the making.

The myth of talent

The concept that people are born with talent or are gifted with it is so blown out of proportion that it's no wonder by the time most kids reach high school they feel they have zero creativity. Don't get me started on grownups.
Sure, there is a tiny handful of people who truly have gifts, but not that many.
I have been accused of being born with this ridiculous fallacy. I can honestly say I find it offensive considering how much work I've done to get where I am. It's a bunch of crap. I don't buy any of it.
You know what talent is? A fuck-ton of elbow-greased-smart-work and dedication channeled selectively at things you need to be skilled at because you are so passionate about them you might curl up and die if you didn't get to do them. And inhale.
You push through freaking worm holes and you crawl over obstacles even when you are paralyzed with fear and hemorrhaging anxiety. That makes talent. That is how you become talented.
I sucked as a writer for a long time. In the last two years I have read well over fifty books on the craft of writing. I watch videos and take online classes. I read everything and anything I can to learn from the best. I edit as if each word will cost me one hundred dollars. And I take my editors' very thoughtful advice with an open heart and a grain of salt, because I trust my instincts. I have the courage to bleed my truths with every story I write and I know I will get criticized regardless. Someday I hope to be a great writer, and then I'll remind myself I know nothing and that I have undiscovered worlds of knowledge to explore.

Blow Your Mind!

Believe in yourself but don't drown in preposterous accolades and puffed up congratulatory BS.
Work like you're a beginner, then grow and evaluate and begin again.

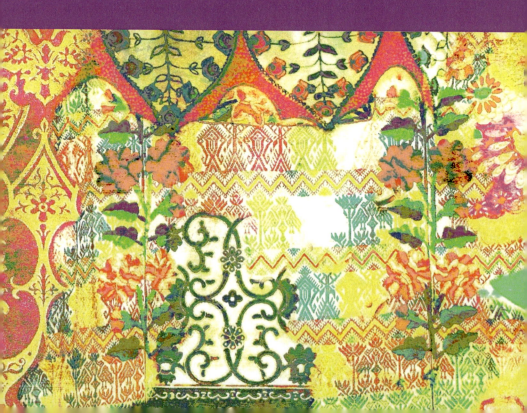

I ALWAYS GO WITH MY CREATIVE WARRIOR.

Desire and need for fierce creativity

How hungry are you? How bad do you want it?
So bad you will do just about anything to live a creative life, and to think more creatively and to approach everything creatively?
Fierce creative? In the marrow of your bones creative?
Sounds glamorous doesn't it. Simple too. I want it, I need it, therefore I shall have it. Gimme, gimme!
It's not that easy. The work is hard. It's really truly hard, and it's not a once and a while thing. It's something you commit to. Every single day.
There's an intensity in being hyper-creative that's like being high. It's the top of the rollercoaster; it's the edge of something most people won't explore. It's a shot of ecstasy in your veins via your brain. The deeper you go the more you see. The more you see the more you crave.
Either you have to have it or you don't. But, it will not be delivered via some magical wish or degree. If you want it that badly you will have to hunt it down and make it your bitch.

WARRIOR THIS

Cancel your subscription to Wishing and Hoping Daily.
Replace it with Unleashing Your Creative Warrior.

THE OCEAN INSIDE YOU IS ENDLESS AND DEEP AND DELICIOUS.

Solitude

I went through a period of time in my late teens when I lived alone in a small apartment in Paris, France.
For a while — when I was working as a barely-making-it model — I lived with seven other models and my boyfriend. Once he left for the States, I lived alone.
I have never in my life felt more alone or lonely than during that time. I'll admit I love being alone. I adore solitude like a drunk likes his drink. I find pure contentment and odd bliss when I'm alone.
Though I loathe loneliness.
To combat the loneliness I created and I read. I ate a lot, too. More pastries than should be legal. Sometimes all I had for dinner was pastries and books. It was so wonderful and gluttonous.
I found myself in the craziness of my solitude.
I learned how beautiful being alone was, and I learned how to overcome many fears.

I learned I could invent worlds via books and creativity, worlds that swept my loneliness into a comforting blanket.

Now with a family of six I appreciate solitude more than ever. Though with the chaos of a full house, I've learned to find myself in the dark hours of the morning and night, but also in the in-betweens. I appreciate the starts and stops of my days, because when my boys come into our studio and look over my shoulder at whatever I'm working on, I know that while they might think I'm a massive weirdo now, someday they'll appreciate that we made a living by creating and that it was a need and a desire.

They will hopefully be reflective enough to want to make sure that however they choose to spend their days it is with colossal desire, gratitude and fierce passion. Oh, and I hope they someday appreciate that solitude can be a gift.

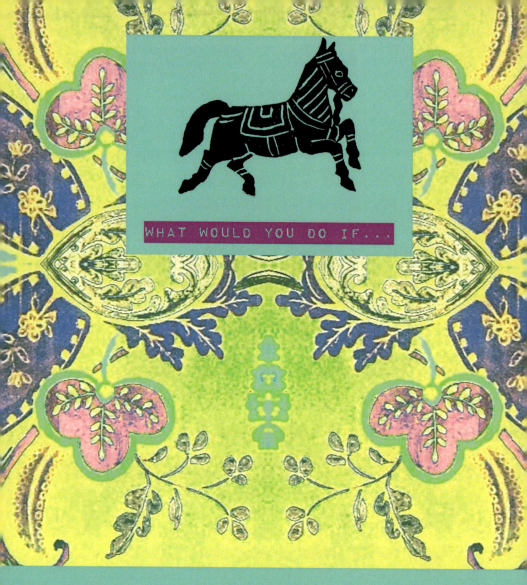

WHAT WOULD YOU DO IF...

You were all alone in your home for one week with no distractions? Does it scare you or inspire you?

On your knees

Ever been there? I have. It's pitiful, shameful, humiliating, discomforting. It's the last place I ever thought I would end up after a long and mostly fruitful career as a designer.

Yes, in the Great Recession we fell flat on our faces and ate dirt big-time. It was our fault. Had we not taken such massive risks – on growth in our company which was going gangbusters – despite all the economic signs around us, we may not have gone bk. We lost more than our company; we lost friends, long-time lovely employees that didn't deserve to go through that, and we lost trust from many people.

It's the ugliest, scariest thing I have ever been through next to my early twenties health issue and infertility.

What did I learn? So much it blows my mind. It alone could be a book.

The following are my blink notes post bk:
- The same people who call you a genius, will call you a moron if you fuck up... to your face, online, and with a knife in your back. So what.
- You will want to die. And you'll have no choice but to move around the hideousness of that obstacle. It is real and stupid and valid. Take action, move on.
- A few angel people will help you, even if you are too afraid to beg. They will help because they've been where you are, and they know that while you have lost temporary faith in yourself, you'll find it again. Truly you will if you take baby steps.
- Many people will abandon you. No one likes a loser. They will flee you in droves. So what. Some of them will come back. Some of them you will never let back in.
- You will be blamed for everything and you will take responsibility. And you will learn and grow from it.
- You will be okay on the other side. You'll be better than okay. You'll be smarter and more hungry than ever.
- People will treat you like a carcass and move in and take whatever they want. So what. They can't take what's inside you and they can't take your creative warrior.
Going through hell may be the greatest thing for one's growth and clarity, and at some point everyone will go through it. Some people will go through it a few times. Just keep moving along.

Practice irresponsible art

once and a while.

Create what you want

This might seem obvious but to many people it's not. I'm going to zero in on writing and art for a second.

When I design my artwork — which eventually becomes a myriad of things from dinnerware to bedding to rugs — I create art I want to live with.

I am fully capable of designing all kinds of different art, and I have done just that for products labeled under generic brands, etc., but it doesn't inspire me like creating art I want to live with.

As for writing, I function the same way. There are lots of trends in writing, most of which don't excite me, so I can't write about them. I have to write stories I want to read.

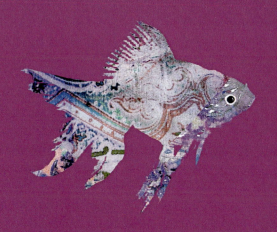

My attention span gets a bit goldfish-like when I read. So if there isn't action from the get-go in a book, I get bored and move on. Same with writing. I like twists, drama, stuff going wrong and crazy things happening. I like breaking then fixing. It's such a blast to write. And I'm certain it's why I can write for hours on end. Sometimes twelve to fifteen hours. Most days I write ten hours, and I write seven days a week. I like it that much.

So when I say create what you want, it makes sense, right? If not, you probably won't be very excited about saddling up to it.

As for trends? I get it, I really do. Many people make a very fine living chasing trends. I often have licensing partners ask me to do it. It's not my bag. I figure there are enough people who do that. I prefer to go my own direction.

WHAT WOULD YOU DO IF...

YOU START TO THINK ABOUT WHAT MIGHT GO RIGHT VERSUS WHAT MIGHT GO WRONG?

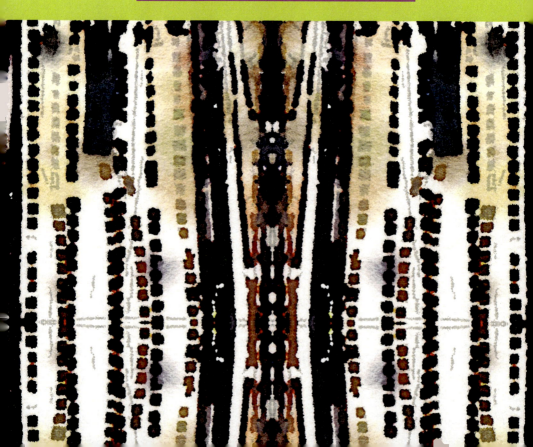

Evolve and fly

Or probably more appropriate, "Don't evolve and die".

Being a creative warrior is about growth and change and being able to do those things regardless of how hard they are.

Every great musician, artist, scientist, teacher, writer will tell you in no uncertain terms you must evolve and grow, or your creative spirit will shrivel into an ugly black curl and slip between the couch cushions along with other dying crumbs.

Sometimes you evolve because you're trying to make a living as a creative and you need to sell more stuff.

Sometimes you evolve because you lost all your tools and you are forced to become a different kind of creator.

And then there are the thousands of other reasons.

Life throws some crazy twists and obstacles at us, and if you cannot bump and groove with those twists, what are you going to do?

Do you really have a choice?

I guess some people do. I don't. I can't afford not to do anything. I have a family and my soul to feed, both of which matter immensely to me. I'm too hungry to not evolve. It might be easier not to evolve if I were a bazillionare and I didn't have to work. But I'm not. If you are too comfy in your life you might struggle a bit more with evolving, because it takes a certain hunger to change. You can find it, but you have to want it real, real bad.

So how does one evolve?

- Stop overthinking since there are few benefits associated with it. Unless you love stewing in anxiety.
- Believe you can. Your mind is powerful, believe and take tiny steps that you are capable.
- Give yourself permission to be you in your truest form.
- Stop defining yourself and just be yourself.
- Take a breather. Look inside. Take micro-action.

Shit will happen.
Be prepared.

Your creative warrior is inside you for a reason.

Use your pain as fuel

Pain is a super real thing everyone is dealing with on some level. Sometimes it's microscopic, sometimes it's mountain massive. Regardless it's there and not something to hide. It's your fucking feelings; they matter for crissake. Use them as fuel.
How?
- You have two choices. Do something or do nothing. Make the right choice.
- Face your pain, in whatever way you need to. Look at yourself in mirror and cry or laugh or yell or write down what hurts. Acknowledge it. It's real. Then take action and make it your fuel. I have created some of my best work as I muddled through pain.
- Grab onto it, then climb inside and use it as a tool. Let it come out in your work. Let go and let it become the soul of your creations. It will help you heal.
- Turn your pain inside out and own it. As much as we hate pain there are many gifts inside it, gifts we don't see until we're on the other side. Trust me I have mined more gifts out of pain than I have out of joy. Joy is great and I live everyday in a bubble of joy because I choose to. But pain happens. No human is immune to it. Either you use it as your bitch, or it uses you.
- Break time into small moments. Allow yourself as much time as you need to use your pain, but commit to using it, commit to action.

Blow Your Mind!

LISTEN TO YOURSELF BEFORE YOU LISTEN TO ANYONE ELSE.

It's not about perfect

It's about doing.
One of the biggest traps in creativity is the idea that you need everything in place before you begin. The right tools, the right environment, the right plan. People run around with their heads cut off trying to gather shit up and make plans of all kinds to ensure what? That things come of flawlessly?
Why? Because they don't want to look stupid or get criticized? Tough luck. If you want to unleash your creative warrior you are going to occasionally look stupid and get criticized. It will happen.
If I hear one more person tell me they have been thinking about painting for the last twenty years but just haven't gotten down to it because they are letting their ideas percolate, I'm going barf, on them, after I had a big bowl of jambalaya, and sangria. You get the point.
Or my other favorite: "I have a book or two in me that I'll write at some point." Then they add in that they have a degree or three in creative writing and journalism and whatever other thing they think is going to help them be a good writer.

You want to know what makes a good creative in any field? A person who sits the fuck down and does the work then evaluates and educates themselves and keeps going regardless of how hard it is some days. And it is hard some days. Count on it.

Perfectionism...

- Kills creativity
- Breeds doubt
- Emphasizes order (another creative buzz kill)
- Increases anxiety
- Is the definitive self-defeating behavior

Stop worrying about perfect and get moving. If you can't tamp down your inner-perfection freak then go organize your sock drawer. I've heard folding socks is trendy, try that.

I don't have time to fold my socks, I'm happily creating.

Blow Your Mind!

TAKE RESPONSIBILITY FOR YOUR THOUGHTS OR THEY WILL CONTROL YOU. MAKE YOUR THOUGHTS YOUR BITCH.

Beautiful messes

There's been a strange "tidy trend" happening over the last few years. I'm not saying tidy is bad. I'm just saying whoa, lighten-the-fuck-up.

You can check out study after study that "tidy tendencies" lead to less creativity. And messy tends to encourage free thinking and higher levels of creativity. (Don't bitch at me, do your own homework! I'm not one of the oodles of scientists who did the studies...)

I cannot work in a pigsty. So I find middle ground. The current trend, in its over-the-top-tidy-ness, makes me feel a bit neurotic (I'll use it as fuel later). Maybe it's because the control freak thing and perfectionism is something I let go a long time ago. It was a stage I went through and I'm rather happy to be on the other side. I accomplished less creatively in my tidy stage because...I was so busy tidying and organizing.

There are so many things that are beautiful about messes:
- They are fun, a little crazy and freeing as all get out.
- Children thrive creatively in messes (so do grownups)
- Messes have no rules. Rules can act like poison and kill creativity.
- You can walk away from messes and come back and jump in again — it's still a mess.
- Messy means risk taking, coloring outside the lines and not being afraid.

WARRIOR THIS

LET GO AND GET MESSY TODAY. IT MIGHT BE THE DETOXIFICATION YOUR INNER PROCRASTINATOR NEEDS.

Sacred spaces

When I was a kid my mom had a small garden room that I hijacked. She was always super supportive of my creativity so she let me use her room as my own. What's amazing is that she never told me I had to clean it up. I loved the messes I made in that room. I learned so much about letting go and exploring and being free. I taught myself many things in that room.
I learned to believe in me, to trust my instincts. And I became a lot of who I am now because of it.
There wasn't anything particularly special about the room besides that it was secluded and had a beautiful view of nature.
I spent a great deal of time creating in that room as it was an escape from the stress of school grades. I might have sucked in school but I rocked in my creative solitude.

I made messes galore that I came back to time and again. I ferreted junk from all drawers in our house and turned that junk into treasures, at least that's what I thought.

From my grandmother, who lived with us, I found in her drawers bits of lace and buttons and other tidbits which became fodder for t-shirts and jackets and jeans. My mom would take me to the craft store downtown once and a while and I would buy random stuff I had no idea how to use. But I figured it out and made all kinds of creations. Sculptures, jewelry and Christmas ornaments and gifts. I loved making and I loved giving things away for free.

A place to create can be a magical thing. It doesn't need to be much but it can bring enormous freedom.

Blow Your Mind!

Need a creative space? Consider...
- A closet. Yes, it doesn't need to be much, just claim it as your own.
- An old camper. I've always wanted a vintage Airstream to create in.
- A shed or a portion of a garage that can be tented off.
- Any room can be divided with bookshelves or a screen or a quilt. Make a creative oasis and get messy.

Do you know how people get stuff done?

They fucking do it.

Use less make more

The idea that we need lots and lots of materials in order to create used to rule my world. It's not that I don't like having access to every kind of tool and substance and texture and scrap of goodness. It's just…I've evolved.
I now look at studios that are crammed with containers and jars of stuff, along with baskets and bins and I wonder how they get to all of it.
My workspace though used to be exactly that.
I suppose when we moved and I had less space to work with I became more cognizant of every square foot. And, I changed how I work. I employ technology much more now. I have fully immersed myself in mobile technology so that I am able to create anywhere in the world at anytime day or night.
I can effortlessly design art while on ski lift or while waiting for one of my kids or while the asparagus steams as were cooking dinner. It's a considerable change to how I used to work.
I now use less to make more. So much more it blows my mind. It has forced my creativity to new levels, and it saves me gobs of money.
I used to be beholden to stacks of magazines and stuff. And computers with graphic programs I didn't know how to use - which meant I had to employ a staff of graphic designers. I no longer have employees, and I love it. The freedom is everything to me.
I am one hundred percent mobile all the time. It's really fun and it allows me to view the whole world as my studio.

REAL IS SEXY

WHAT WOULD YOU DO IF...

You could only use one tool? Could you still create? Would you create more freely?
- You lived on a boat half the year? What would you need to be a creative warrior?
- You had no team? (some have teams, some don't)
- You lost one of your most important creative senses? This last one I'll admit scares the crap out of me.

Turn ingratitude inside out

Being grateful is another one of those cool free things in life that seems impossible not to want. Not only is it free, it's not elusive. Anyone can have it at anytime.
It's better for you than most anything in the world and it gives back. There is zero downside and gigantic upside.
Are you harnessing it? Or are you overthinking how to get it.
Take some action and it'll be yours.
Humility is part of it. Not the meek kind where you don't matter. Trust me, you matter. I'm speaking more to the everything-isn't-about-you kind. This sort of goes back to my thoughts on the idea that the universe isn't revolving around me and that I shouldn't get bummed out when my cosmic alignment (or whatever) isn't answering all the wishes I blew into the wind.

I'm humble enough to know nothing will happen unless I dream it, and then do it. For me that is where grateful begins. It's a very personal thing and we all arrive at it in our own good time and in our own spiritual boats. Gratitude tends to be grounded in reason. Typically you arrive at it after a string of trials and tribulations. Perspective can offer a set of powerful wings to fly in on. Loss, pain, fear, joy, and/or change can all provide the appropriate nudges toward the wisdom of being grateful.
The things being grateful will bring are endless - here is a tiny appetizer list.
- Better health
- Bounce back when you need it
- Optimism
- Self-belief
- Friends and family that crave your presence
- Spiked endorphins
- Explosive happiness
- Anxiety relief

Blow Your Mind!

Add to this list. Make it personal and be specific about what you are grateful for and what being more grateful can bring not just to you, but to those you love.

Using nature as your mentor

Nature is the greatest adapter there is. This is pretty cool if you think about it. It refuses to be trapped. It adapts up or around or under everything. It evolves nonstop. Every day, every season. The only time it goes backward is if humans mutilate it or it dies by natural causes. And even when we mutilate it, it finds a way to keep growing. It's that powerful.

Nature is the greatest creative warrior there is.

It says grow, adjust, progress or die. Being fluid is part of the joy of being alive. It's what makes learning new skills and exploring ones creativity so much fucking fun.

I was brave enough.

And that is everything.

WHAT WOULD YOU DO IF...

You created and lived by a new vocabulary?
Wild, free, messy, beautiful, believing, loving, joyful, delicious, brave, courageous….
Burn your old vocabulary. You won't need it once you unleash your creative warrior.

The beauty in fear

I believe fear exists to help us. It exists so we can learn how to move around it, dive into it, face it and grow from it.
The feeling of fear is as powerful as gratitude, and it will drive you closer to true gratitude if you don't let it cage you.
Yes, it takes introspection and guts and a whole lot of fuck-this-shit, because it's real, and it can exist in dark or light, in stupidity or intelligence, and in any age or race or culture.
It can be your bully or your saint. I hate it. I loathe the sonofabitch but then I make it my saint.
It can tear you down, or it can be your mountain to climb. It's a choice. A hard one, but it is a choice.
Fear is a gift. It will make your heart pound. It will make you dizzy and breathless – like love, but it will awaken you. Invigorate you. Push you.
Unless you let it cripple you.
Your creative warrior might just be your best defense against fear. This might hurt a little, but you will heal and grow and learn. No one is fearless. Some people are just better at looking fear in the face and using it to help them move forward.

Let others see the real you.

Blow Your Mind!

Write down your fears and your creative warrior actions. A few examples:
• Fear of being average – create in truth
• Fear of being rejected – the more you create and evaluate and learn and grow the more skilled you will become. Fear lessens as you gain confidence.
• Fear of failure – the only failure is not doing. Doing and taking action will lead to something. Not doing is nothingness. Fear loves people who do nothing – they are soul food for fear.

There is no gatekeeper,
no relation, no God.

It's yours to own.
CREATIVITY!

The End Game

Where are you going creatively? Why worry about it...just go.

Invent a new world that is limitless, where you unleash your creative warrior nonstop. We have zero control over the unknown and if you let go of the idea that you cannot steer your ship in the exact direction you think it ought to go then the journey will be that much more gratifying.

The number one most important take away from this book is to take action. Action can conquer fear and anxiety, self-doubt and so forth. Unleashing your creative warrior is a very doable thing, with smart and hard work, persistence, courage and hunger it can happen. Not easily. Not in five seconds, but eventually, yes, it can happen.

But will you make it happen? Now it's up to you.

P.S. I believe you can. I'm rooting for you xxx

The following is that "about me" section I warned you about earlier.

About Me

Why trust me?
Don't, if you want perfect

Academically I was a 'C' student. I failed more than one class in high school. Written tests and memorization skills were my greatest downfalls. I was a creative. It's where I thrived. And sadly that's still at the bottom of the list when it comes to our current academic environment.

To be clear, I'm pro-Math, -Science and -English. But everything should be couched in creativity. EVERYTHING!

Scared stiff of failure, I skipped over the entire math section on my SAT's, and was told afterwards by one of my favorite teachers that I would never be successful in life. ("in life"?? 'cuz I skipped a section of the SAT's? I don't think so.)

Luckily, my parents told me "success" came in all sizes, shapes and colors. Just like people. My parents were – and still are – the absolute bomb.

Thankfully, I loved making all kinds of things and my parents encouraged it, as they saw it bring me confidence where my grades often crushed me to my core.

Four days after graduation from high school I was gone. I won a modeling contest in New York and a ticket to Paris to boot. I crossed the pond to explore whatever Europe had to offer and give modeling a shot.

I had no idea at the time that I was entering entrepreneur boot camp. Modeling is not entrepreneurship but I was on an accelerated course of sales, marketing, constant re-invention and learning how to package me. I was humbled and then some, time and again. "No" was my constant reminder that I was not special. I was continually told I was not exceptional in any way, time and again. I was told that I needed a nose job, a boob job, have my ears pinned back, grow two inches, create a waist, wear hazel contact lenses and be someone, or something I wasn't. Demoralization wasn't just a code word; it was how I lived for almost two years. Thanks to my strong spine, I said no to all of their requests to change me, the best product I had. All the while, I continued to make things – craft things, or develop products – on the side.
    I'd sew clothes, decorate shoes with vintage junk jewels, paint silk scarves and craft jewelry. I'd troll scrap yards for supplies, then turn odd old bits into funky home furnishings. This was my passion; this was my calling. It made me happy. But could it be my purpose? Could I have a career making things?
    Most people told me to narrow my focus and take some classes, maybe get a degree to solve my dilemma. I was often advised to consider the practical applications of art, such as

architecture or graphic design. Something that could lead to a real job. (dancing in my head all during that time was 'fuck that; I got this. I just need to focus and move forward.)

  I had always thought art school would be an incredible journey to explore, though I always assumed I would never be able to get in based on my crappy high school grades.

  I was mostly right. Even art schools wanted kids who tested well on their SAT's. But, after much conversation, negotiating, and working my tail off on a portfolio to make a good impression on the admissions folks, The Art Institute of Chicago permitted me to hand over a mammoth wad of cash and enroll in a few classes. Man, was I stoked!

  I pulled ten thousand dollars out of my hard earned savings account and handed it over to these folks with more belief in the system than I should have had. I thought and assumed I was investing in me. But only a few months in it didn't feel like it was about my education so much as it was about their system.

  I was certain college was going to kill my creativity and spirit. I was chomping at the bit for more, and too hungry to stay. So after trying out a few classes, and feeling nothing but duped, I walked away. One of my professors offered to buy my class project; I gave it to her.

A month later, at the age of twenty, realizing limits are bullshit and that I had nothing to lose, I started my first business. Though it was short-lived, I learned a good deal about my truths, and grit, plus a little about what it takes to make your passion purposeful. But the most important thing I learned was a shit-ton about explosive happiness, and how I wasn't going to live any other way.

At twenty-three, I married my favorite person. Twenty-five years later I still know it was the right choice. Together we've started eight companies. Family, friends, employees and investors all helping things progress as we grew.

We have designed everything, from apparel, shoes and jewelry to tableware, fabric, sinks, furniture, rugs, lighting, wall art and more. How? Because we believed we could, then we took micro-steps to make things happen. We didn't just dream, we DID. There is a big fat hairy difference.

We've written almost twenty books, on topics ranging from home decorating to entertaining to sexy erotic romance novels.

We have sold our designs to the largest retailers in the world: Target, Costco, Bed Bath and Beyond, Macy's, Bloomingdales, Nordstrom, Neiman Marcus, QVC, HSN and so forth. We've been retailers, manufacturers, importers, boot-strappers and everything in-between-ers.

I've been awarded puffed-up accolades that could easily make an ego swell. And some years it really did, paired with failures.

I've been called a star entrepreneur, a trail-blazing retailer and an iconoclastic designer. I've also been called a loser, an idiot, a failure, and an uneducated disgrace.

After going bankrupt in the Great Recession, I was shamed and humiliated as we lost so many investors', customers' and friends' capital, and worse...their trust.

We had to let go lovely long-time friends and wonderful creative employees that helped us build everything by faithfully working their tails off year after year with incredible dedication.

It was a disappointing conclusion following years of growing, failing up, and accomplishing.

I never cried so much, or felt more despair.

Embarrassed didn't begin to describe what we went through. No one was to blame but us. I am more certain than ever that this is true. We should have been better at calculating risk. We should have seen the economic fall coming. But, everything we did proved, time and again, we were bullet-proof. Everyone around us — businesses that had a vested stake in our success — encouraged us to let it ride. Our bankers, our vendors and our consultants.

We bought all that bullshit. Then we ate it. We pushed all of our cards onto the table, and we lost. My god, how we lost.
    And honestly, so much more than money. We lost faith and hope and friends - relationships that really mattered.
    We lost confidence and belief in our creativity, and in ourselves.
What's truly amazing is that my husband, John, and I didn't lose each other.
    Now, on the other side of the calamity, we can identify what went wrong and why. Well, sort of.
    I never thought I'd say I was grateful we went through that shit-storm, but I am. We were forced to change everything. We had to dig deep and dissect what we wanted to become next and why.
    There have been scores of bumps, bruises and skinned knees, but our ego's are more in check than ever. Plus, we know now — better than ever — that bumps are part of the deal. It's how you work through them and learn from them and push forward that really matters.
    We learned that recreating oneself might be as essential as air. We live by it.

Thanks again for reading this, the second book in the Make It Your Bitch series. The other two are available on Amazon: Unearthing Your Passion & Purpose To Find Explosive Happiness and Notes for Creating A Happy Enchanting Soulful Home.

Please take a minute to leave your review on Amazon for Unleashing Your Creative Warrior — reviews are everything to the self-published author and we value your input and perspective more than we can tell you.

For my romance novels, please check out www.awildingwells.com

To see the world of Poetic Wanderlust, please go to www.poeticwanderlust.com

I really appreciate you taking the time to read this far. Lastly, please join our mailing list at poeticwanderlust.com.

Cheers,

Tracy

Ta!

Made in the USA
San Bernardino, CA
25 October 2016